1776

A NEW LOOK AT
REVOLUTIONARY
WILLIAMSBURG

1776

A NEW LOOK AT REVOLUTIONARY WILLIAMSBURG

BY K. M. KOSTYAL

with

Colonial Williamsburg®

THE COLONIAL WILLIAMSBURG FOUNDATION

PHOTOGRAPHS BY LORI EPSTEIN RENDA

NATIONAL GEOGRAPHIC

WASHINGTON, D.C.

*Costumed interpreters—
trained role players who portray
18th-century people—stroll
through Colonial Williamsburg's
historic area.*

Table of Contents

FOREWORD   6

INTRODUCTION: A REVOLUTIONARY CITY   8

VIRGINIA'S COLONIAL CAPITAL   10

Virginia's Indians   16

A NEW SPIRIT   18

REVOLUTION!   22

Virginia's Declaration of Rights   26

THE CITY AT WAR   28

Reading History's Clues   36

A HARD-WON VICTORY   38

CONCLUSION: BIRTH OF A NATION   42

Bringing the Past to Life/Portraying a Slave   44

Chronology ❧ Index   46

Foreword

Cathleene B. Hellier, Historian
The Colonial Williamsburg Foundation

The Colonial Williamsburg Foundation operates the world's largest "living history" museum—the restored 18th-century capital of Virginia, Britain's largest and wealthiest American colony. If you visit Williamsburg, you can see hundreds of buildings that look just as they did when our nation was young. You can meet real people dressed as people did in the 1770s and see how they lived and worked. You can hear their stories that bring history to life. There are even opportunities for you to experience Revolutionary life for yourself.

At Colonial Williamsburg, history is also "living" in another way. Our understanding of what happened in the past is always changing. Historians are always discovering new things, and this book presents many of those new discoveries about the people who lived in Williamsburg. You can now meet a much more diverse group of costumed interpreters—men and women, rich and poor, black and white and Native American, slave and indentured and free.

And you can see how their lives changed dramatically in 1776, when Americans declared their independence from Great Britain. When the long, difficult war for independence was over, the people of Williamsburg—and America—were no longer subjects of a king. They were Americans, the people of a new nation.

The eight-sided brick Magazine, where military equipment was stored, was the site of tensions between the patriots and the royal governor. It held enough guns and ammunition to supply a small army.

INTRODUCTION:
A REVOLUTIONARY CITY

The small town of Williamsburg played a very large role in the American Revolution. Because of this, Williamsburg's revolutionary spirit has long been associated with the most famous of revolutionaries—our nation's Founding Fathers—George Washington, Thomas Jefferson, and Patrick Henry. Other people associate Williamsburg during the Revolution with another image: members of the town's gentry in their fine clothes and powdered wigs enjoying elegant dinners or dancing the minuet. These images are true, but the life of Williamsburg's residents was much more varied than that.

Historians now know that at the time of the Revolution, more than half of colonial Williamsburg's residents were enslaved African Virginians. Even though they spent their days working for their white masters, they had families, traditions, and dreams of their own. Historians are trying to piece those lives together. A new online database that tracks the voyages of slave ships from Africa to America will help us better understand what parts of Africa certain enslaved people came from and what traditions they brought with them.

Historians also now know that Williamsburg was a fluid society, where new immigrants from Europe came and went. It was also a society affected by those who made Williamsburg their permanent home. A few Indian boys attended a school established at the College of William and Mary to "civilize" them. Williamsburg in the 18th century was a multicultural city.

Today, Colonial Williamsburg's interpreters bring to life colonial times. They present the joys and hardships of enslaved African Virginians, the public and private lives of the gentry, and the cares and hopes of farmers who lived on the edge of the small but dynamic world that was colonial Williamsburg.

During the Revolution, American soldiers poured into Williamsburg at different times. The townspeople were glad to have their protection, but the soldiers also disrupted life in the little burg.

VIRGINIA'S COLONIAL CAPITAL

*I*t had been a struggle to keep the English colony of Virginia alive when it was first established in the early 1600s. The colonists' settlement, Jamestown, was in the marshy wilderness along the James River, an ocean away from the comforts of their homes in England. But once the settlers found they could grow tobacco and sell it to Europe, the colony began to thrive. More people came to Virginia, some starting small farms, others creating vast plantations along the river.

Jamestown continued to be the colony's only town and capital until 1698, when its statehouse burned down for the fourth time. Then, in 1699, the colony's elected representatives, called burgesses, passed an "Act Directing the Building of the Capitoll and the City of Williamsburgh," named in honor of King William III.

Middle Plantation, a settlement at the site for the new capital, was located on a peninsula between the James and York Rivers. It was threaded by deep creeks that made it easy to transport goods by boat, and it had springs to provide water for drinking. The capital site already had two important institutions, the new College of William and Mary and Bruton Parish Church.

Williamsburg's broad main street, named for the Duke of Gloucester, ran from the College of William and Mary past homes and shops to the colonial Capitol (opposite), where the British flag flew as a sign of empire. Free and enslaved townsfolk came to the town's Market Square (above) on market days. Meat, fish, live chickens and other fowl, eggs, milk, vegetables, and fruit were for sale.

Williamsburg's broad main street, Duke of Gloucester Street, ran almost a mile through the heart of town. Unpaved, it was muddy when it rained and dusty when it didn't and was scattered with the dung of horses and other animals. In the first few years, not many lots of land were sold, and Williamsburg grew so slowly that one colonist called it an "imaginary City."

Gradually, beginning about 1710, Williamsburg began to grow. Along Duke of Gloucester Street, merchants opened shops selling goods from England, and government officials and families from the wealthy gentry, who owned plantations in the countryside, built fine homes for themselves in town. One visitor described Duke of Gloucester Street as "one of the most spacious in North-America."

While wealthy gentry women enjoyed tea and other leisurely activities, their slaves waited on them. Enslaved children and adults worked long days with little reward.

Several days a week, the town's Market Square was crowded with carts filled with eggs, meat, milk, oysters, fish, and produce for sale. Four times a year Virginia's highest courts held sessions in the Capitol, filling the town and taverns with people from throughout the colony.

More and more immigrants from England, Scotland, and other parts of Europe settled in the town. These new arrivals were hardworking and anxious to create good lives for themselves. But many of Williamsburg's immigrants had not come to town willingly. They came as slaves.

Historians used to believe that the first African immigrants to America came as indentured servants, just as many white people did. In order to earn their freedom, these servants had to work a number of years for the masters who had paid their ship's passage. But new research indicates that even those first blacks often served for life, and their children inherited this slave status from them.

In West Africa, men and women were captured to be brought to the New World and sold in the inhumane slave trade. By studying ships' logs, historians estimate that about four out of every five women who crossed the Atlantic during colonial times were African. Many Africans—men and women—died in the crossing, crowded like cargo into the holds of slave ships. The ones who survived arrived in a world completely foreign to them and spent the rest of their lives in long daily labor.

These enslaved humans had no legal right to participate in the dream of a better life for themselves or their children. Yet their labor contributed to the comfort and wealth of many white residents. Very few slaves could read or write at this time, so they left little record of how they felt about their enslavement. One letter, though, written by a "poor Slave" in Virginia in 1723 to a bishop in London, pled with him to "Releese us out of this Cruell Bondegg." The world inhabited by enslaved residents in the new Virginia capital was very different from the one inhabited by white townsfolk.

For Sale:
A young healthy Negro Wench, who is an exceeding fine Spinner, can wash and iron well, and do other Business in a family, likewise her child. For further particulars inquire of messrs. Dixon and Hunter

Journeyman Gunsmiths and Blacksmiths will meet with

Slaves could be sold by their owners (above) at any time, and any child born to an enslaved woman was also a slave and "belonged" to her master. Both white and black citizens attended Bruton Parish Church (below), though blacks did so only if their masters approved.

By 1760 Williamsburg was a well-established town. Though the townsfolk were not all British by birth, they were still British subjects who bought British goods in the shops, observed British laws, and lived with the royal governor as their neighbor. One of the young men at the College of William and Mary, Virginia-born Thomas Jefferson, remembered dining with the governor: "At these dinners I have heard more good sense, more rational and philosophical conversations, than in all my life besides."

Still, the New World was a long way from the mother country, and different from it. In America people were less confined to social classes. Virginia certainly had a wealthy class, called the gentry, but the "middling sort," as they were called—the merchants and artisans (or craftspeople) of Williamsburg and the small farmers on the outskirts of town—could become wealthier and move up in social status. In Europe that was difficult to do. Some in the middle levels of society could afford to buy the kinds of things the gentry bought—specialized home furnishings and stylish clothing. "Pride of wealth is as ostentatious in this country as ever the pride of birth has been elsewhere," wrote one English visitor.

The 13 Colonies in 1776

BRITISH NORTH AMERICA

MASS. (DISTRICT OF MAINE)
NEW HAMPSHIRE
NEW YORK
MASSACHUSETTS
RHODE ISLAND
PENNSYLVANIA
CONNECTICUT
NEW JERSEY
DELAWARE
VIRGINIA   MARYLAND
NORTH CAROLINA
ATLANTIC OCEAN
GEORGIA
SOUTH CAROLINA

0   mi   200

N.Y.
PA.
OHIO
MD.
N.J.
W. VA.
DEL.
KY.
Williamsburg
VIRGINIA
TENN.
N.C.
Atlantic Ocean
GA.
S.C.
Present-day boundaries are shown.

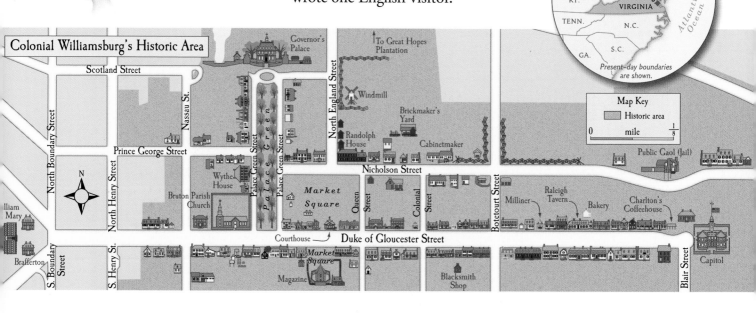

Colonial Williamsburg's Historic Area

Scotland Street
Governor's Palace
To Great Hopes Plantation
Windmill
Brickmaker's Yard

North Boundary Street
Nassau St.
North England Street
Randolph House
Cabinetmaker

Prince George Street
Public Gaol (Jail)

Map Key
Historic area
0   mile   1/8

Wythe House
Bruton Parish Church
Palace Green
Palace Green Street
Market Square
Queen Street
Nicholson Street
Colonial Street
Botetourt Street
Milliner
Raleigh Tavern
Bakery
Charlton's Coffeehouse

N

North Henry Street
William Mary
Brafferton
S. Boundary Street
S. Henry St.

Courthouse
Duke of Gloucester Street
Market Square
Magazine
Blacksmith Shop
Blair Street
Capitol

Among the status symbols, of course, were slaves. Their hard work often accounted for their white owners' prosperity, while they themselves never would be prosperous. The one good thing that Williamsburg offered its black residents was a school for their children. The Bray School opened in 1760, but the masters of enslaved children had to give their consent for children to attend. Often students missed school because they were needed for other work. The school focused on the teachings of the Anglican Church, but it also taught children to read and write—an invaluable skill they could pass on to other African Virginians and use to their own advantage.

For one thing, being able to write meant a slave had a better chance to escape to freedom. Whenever slaves traveled on errands, they had to carry a pass from their masters saying they had permission to be on their own. By studying reward notices for runaway slaves placed in the *Virginia Gazette,* historians now know that slaves who could write might forge such passes and flee. One of these notices in 1771 described a runaway slave named Peter as "an artful smooth talkative Fellow, can read and write, and may probably have a forged Pass." Those skills may have been Peter's keys to freedom.

A cobbler, one of Williamsburg's artisans, sits in his shop making shoes. Women's shoes were fabric and men's shoes were made from leather.

Virginia's Indians

What Europeans called the New World was hardly new to the native peoples who had lived in North America for thousands of years. But in just a few decades, the colonists had forced them off their land. Only about 2,000 Powhatan Indians were left in coastal Virginia when Williamsburg was founded. A few lived near towns and adopted the lifestyle of the colonists. Others lived more traditional lives in villages in the countryside. Many of them sold pottery, wooden bowls and spoons, and fish and wild game to the townspeople. Some Indians in early Virginia were captured in wars and forced to become slaves.

When the College of William and Mary began, young Indian boys were invited to live at the school and learn the subjects that the "best Englishmen's sons do learn." Some of the boys who came died, often from diseases that were new to them.

In 1723 the Brafferton School was built at the college especially to educate Indian boys. Parents at first worried that instead of being educated, their children might be sold into slavery. In the 54 years it operated, the Brafferton educated only about 110 Indians. The British hoped the boys would return to their tribes, convert their people to Christianity, and teach them European ways, but only a few straddled both worlds. Instead, when most of the children returned home, their elders often complained that "they were neither fit for hunters, warriors, nor councilors; they were totally good for nothing."

Cherokee Indians, who lived well southwest of Williamsburg, maintained their power and traditions longer than other tribes in the Southeast. Their emissaries came to negotiate with the royal governor, and the governor's emissaries also visited the Cherokee (background).

A New Spirit

As the mid-1700s progressed and America became more established, British officials began to feel that the colonists should help pay some of the expenses of administering the colonies. In the spring of 1765, the British Parliament enacted the Stamp Act. It placed a stamp tax on things like the colonists' newspapers and legal documents, even dice and playing cards.

Throughout the 13 colonies—the 13 divisions of British America—a cry of protest went up. The colonists had no representatives of their own in Parliament, so this was taxation without representation. In the Capitol in Williamsburg, one of the members of the House of Burgesses gave a speech against the king, George III. Patrick Henry's language was so fiery and threatening that other burgesses shouted "Treason!"

A year later, Parliament repealed the Stamp Act, but soon new taxes followed. As Englishmen, the colonists had thought they were the freest people in the world. Now they were beginning to doubt that and to distrust first Parliament and then the king. They realized the colonies needed to cooperate in a way they never had. Virginians suggested Committees of Correspondence—

Opposite: At night the enslaved families of Williamsburg laid whatever rags or other bedding they could find on the floors of kitchens or attics to sleep. They had no space to call their own and very few belongings. Above: One of the fiercest voices against the British was Virginian Patrick Henry, whose speeches have gone down in history.

When Lord Dunmore, the royal governor, ordered British sailors to sneak gunpowder out of the Magazine in 1775, angry townspeople threatened to attack the Governor's Palace. Prominent citizens talked them out of the assault.

information-sharing bodies that would allow all of the legislatures of different colonies to communicate with one another directly.

It was a first step in uniting the colonies and it came at a good time, because in May 1773 a new law related to tea upset the colonists. It led to the Boston Tea Party when protesters dumped tea into Boston Harbor in objection to the tax and in defense of their rights as Englishmen. The next year the colonists took another step toward uniting against the British. They held the first Continental Congress in Philadelphia. A leading citizen of Williamsburg, Peyton Randolph, was elected president, and members voted to stop trading with Britain.

In Williamsburg, the king's representative in Virginia, royal governor Lord Dunmore, dissolved Virginia's House of Burgesses to suppress disloyalty. In the spring of 1775, its elected leaders met anyway—in Richmond instead of Williamsburg—as the Virginia Convention. Again, Patrick Henry delivered a passionate speech: "The next gale that sweeps from the north will bring to our ears the clash of resounding arms! . . . I know not what course others may take; but as for me, give me Liberty or give me Death!"

People sympathetic to Britain could be coated with hot tar (in the cask, left) and feathers (in the bag, right), a painful procedure.

Not all colonists shared Henry's rebellious ideas. Many loyal British subjects could not imagine turning against their king and country. Some moved out of Williamsburg to farms or plantations. Others moved back to England, taking their families and possibly a household slave with them. That slave would never see his or her friends and family in Virginia again.

The more independent the Virginians became, the less Lord Dunmore liked it. Under his orders, British sailors sneaked several barrels of gunpowder out of the Magazine in Williamsburg, the place where powder was stored, before dawn on April 21, 1775. The citizens of Williamsburg were furious, and a mob gathered to make sure no more powder was taken. Dunmore threatened to arm the slaves against the mob.

At about the same time, British and colonial troops met in battle in the Massachusetts towns of Lexington and Concord. Patrick Henry had been right. The gale from the north had brought the clash of arms. Whether they were ready for it or not, the colonists had begun their revolution against the mother country.

Families were torn apart by the coming Revolution. When Loyalists returned to England, many of their slaves were sold to new owners, separating them from friends and family.

REVOLUTION!

In the spring of 1775 tensions between Lord Dunmore and the citizens of Williamsburg reached a breaking point. The governor said that he was "threatened every night with an assault" from the angry citizens, so he slipped away from the city and boarded a ship on the nearby York River. He didn't sail away, though. He watched from shipboard, planning what to do with the rebellious patriots. In Williamsburg, patriots and royal officials nearly came to blows over gunpowder in the Magazine. The colonists thought that they, not the British, had a right to it. They knew they needed it to defend themselves.

In Philadelphia the second Continental Congress appointed Virginian George Washington as commander in chief of the Continental forces. He was given the huge job of organizing and training an army that could fight Britain, the most powerful country in the world.

On August 23, 1775, King George proclaimed the American colonies in rebellion. War had come quickly, and in so many ways the patriots weren't prepared for it. To make matters worse, a violent hurricane struck the East Coast, with "prodigious flows that drive vast sheets of rain before it, and makes everything shake almost to their foundations," one Virginian man reported. The storm became known as the Independence Hurricane.

When the first Virginia patriots came forward to fight the British, there was no organized army at all and no standard uniform (opposite). Most men had served only in local militias, formed to protect their communities from danger. Williamsburg's blacksmiths increased gun production (tools shown above). Rifles and bayonets were the most important weapons of the war.

Enslaved people all over Williamsburg whispered about whether they should take advantage of Lord Dunmore's offer—their freedom in exchange for fighting the patriots.

Meanwhile, Lord Dunmore was waging war against the Virginians. In November, he issued a decree that all slaves owned by Virginia's patriots would be freed if they joined His Majesty's forces. This was an opportunity no enslaved Virginian had ever dreamed of. All over Williamsburg slaves whispered together as they worked. Could they trust the British to keep their word? Should they leave behind the world they knew and their friends and families to take this risk for freedom? In the end, several hundred decided to fight with the British.

Soldiers came into Williamsburg after the war began, and by fall of 1775, almost 2,000 were encamped around town. They more than doubled the town's population. The soldiers lacked weapons, ammunition, and uniforms. Many brought their own tomahawks and hunting knives and wore hunting shirts, so the British later called them "shirt men."

Soon, fences were being torn down to feed soldiers' fires, and troops marched in the streets.

As fighting with the British broke out in new areas, an idea began to grow among the patriots. Maybe what was really needed was independence from Britain. This was a huge step. The colonists had always seen themselves as part of Britain, and they relied on it for so much. It required a lot of courage to make a break with the mother country.

Meeting in Williamsburg in May 1776, Virginia's patriot leaders decided that at the next Continental Congress in Philadelphia "the United Colonies" should declare themselves "free and independent States." From atop the Virginia Capitol, the British flag was lowered and replaced by the Grand Union flag of Washington's army. Townsfolk celebrated with parades and lights.

In early June, Virginia's proposal was presented to the Continental Congress. On July 4, the Declaration of Independence, written mostly by Virginia delegate Thomas Jefferson, was accepted.

News traveled slowly in the 1700s, only as fast as horses, ships, and humans could carry it. It took a couple weeks for word of the Declaration of Independence to reach Williamsburg. Not until July 25 did a prominent citizen stand in front of the courthouse and read the declaration's now famous words to a gathered crowd: "We hold these truths to be self-evident, that all men are created equal, that they are endowed by their Creator with certain unalienable Rights, that among these are Life, Liberty and the pursuit of Happiness."

Despite the beauty of the language, it didn't truly apply to all people. Slaves, Indians, and women were denied those promised rights—as were all those who didn't own property. Still, the colonies had defied Britain and declared their independence. Now they would have to fight a long, hard war to win it permanently.

Above: The Declaration of Independence was read aloud to the citizens of Williamsburg on July 25, 1776. Below: In dangerous times, pistols like this were carried by civilians when they traveled.

ORDINA

A DECLARATION of RIG

the good people of Virginia, a∫

which rights do pertain to them,

foundation of government.

1. THAT all men are by na
and have certain inhe
enter into a ∫tate of ∫ociety, they
or dive∫t their po∫terity; namely
with the means of acquiring and
and obtaining happine∫s and ∫afe

2. That all power is ve∫ted i
the people; that magi∫trates are
all times amenable to them.

3. That government is, or
common benefit, protection, ar
or community of all the vario

Virginia's Declaration of Rights

In the spring of 1776, while the Second Continental Congress was meeting in Philadelphia, the Virginia Convention was meeting in Williamsburg. Its delegates were trying to decide what rights Virginians should have, now that British law was no longer the law of the land. George Mason took the lead in drafting a document to declare those rights. The Virginia document began, "All men are by nature equally free and independent, and have certain inherent rights." Did that mean slaves, too? one convention member asked. No, others said, it did not.

On June 12, 1776, the Virginia Convention adopted Mason's Declaration of Rights. It proclaimed that the right to govern comes from the people themselves, not from a king or other higher power. It also said that government should serve the people, and people should elect their representatives to government. A new constitution said government should be divided into three branches—legislative, executive, and judicial. The declaration promised freedom of the press and religion and trial by jury, as well as other rights.

Much of what was in the Virginia declaration would later become the foundation for the Constitution's Bill of Rights, which was drafted in 1789 and ratified, or signed into law, in 1791.

The Virginia Declaration of Rights (background) was the work of the fifth Virginia Convention, the same group of people who instructed their delegates to the Continental Congress to propose independence.

THE CITY AT WAR

During the first years of the Revolution, most of the fighting took place in the north, near Philadelphia and New York. Lord Dunmore and his forces left Virginia in the summer of 1776 and went to New York to join other redcoats, as the Americans called the British. That same summer, the Virginia troops camped around Williamsburg grew restless and began to lose discipline. Some stole from farms near town, while others gambled or shot off their guns for no reason. By late summer, though, most were on the way north to join the Continental Army and George Washington.

The people of Williamsburg were probably glad to have more order restored to their lives, but they also worried the town could be easily attacked without troops to protect it. And families that had sent their husbands and sons off to fight worried about their safety.

The war also left townspeople with fewer of the things they needed. The cost of bacon, sugar, and salt climbed higher and higher, as the war disrupted trade. Shops that depended on imported goods had to close.

Many of the items townspeople used in their homes—from paint to clothes to candles to soap to tea—came from trade with Britain. Now Virginians had to make those things

---

With the coming of the Revolution, merchants who relied on British goods,
like this milliner (opposite), could no longer get the wares they needed to stay in business
and had to close their shops. But the town's blacksmiths (above) made more of the items
the townspeople and Continental Army needed.

During the Revolution, a black preacher named Gowan Pamphlet helped the enslaved people of Williamsburg form their own church for the first time.

themselves or go without, so soap and candle factories opened on the edge of town. Some of Williamsburg's artisans, like the blacksmith and the wheelwright, began supplying the Continental Army, and their businesses prospered.

In the first year of the war, the Virginia General Assembly met in Williamsburg. Working with the new governor, Patrick Henry, it established laws and ways of administering Virginia, to take the place of the old British system. At first the government was not ready for war, and its operations were inefficient and slow, sometimes hampering the war effort.

Virginians took pride in the fact that their delegates were elected by the "people." What that really meant was that white men who owned land were allowed to vote, not women, blacks, Indians, or poor white men. Still, it was an improvement over Britain, where only a small percentage of men could vote. And it was a first step toward a democratic republic.

By this time more than half of Williamsburg's residents were black. The war years were hard for them. They were the ones who suffered most from the shortages, which affected even the wealthiest households. Lean times may have led masters to sell their slaves more readily, which could separate families forever.

About this time, black preachers began gathering their own followers. They didn't have churches, so they often held services outside and delivered sermons that had messages about equality and freedom embedded in them. Like other Virginians, African Virginians worried about who would win the war and how the war's end might change their lives. One thing was certain—the independence and freedom that white Americans thought was their birthright and worth fighting for wouldn't be extended to black Americans.

Even though some of Williamsburg's black residents could write, historians have uncovered little written by them during the colonial period, especially details about their personal lives. They have to tease out those details

Left: Young white girls were taught how to take care of a household, so that when they became wives and mothers they would know what to do. Part of their training included how to manage slaves and servants.

Below: At Great Hopes Plantation on the edge of town, as on many small farms, owners and slaves lived and worked close together. Larger plantations had many more slaves and separate living quarters for them.

from things whites wrote about African Virginians. But even in the diaries and letters of the white townspeople, there are few details of personal life. Most of us don't record in our diaries what we wear or eat for dinner or when we brush our teeth. But those are the daily details historians would like to understand better.

In August 1777, an "alarm and bustle" spread through Williamsburg, when people heard that a British fleet was in the Chesapeake Bay. From all over Virginia, troops marched toward Williamsburg and the vicinity, and by late August, 4,000 soldiers had gathered.

In late October the townsfolk received good news. The Continental Army had scored a big victory against the British

Opposite: Black and white children who lived in the same household often spent their early years as playmates, but once they reached their teens, the relationship changed to that of master and slave.

Even though the Revolution brought soldiers—both British and Continental—to Williamsburg, children often went on with their lives, playing bat-and-ball (above) and other games. Below: Gourds dry in the sun at Great Hopes Plantation.

Shoes at the time were made of all kinds of leathers, even goat hide. With no running water, chamber pots could be found in every bedroom.

at Saratoga, New York. The city celebrated with a parade. Bells rang, and candles and torches lit up streets. A few months later in early 1778, more welcome news arrived—France had agreed to join the war as an ally of the Americans!

Still, the war dragged on year after year. Williamsburg wasn't directly affected by it very often, but in 1779 a notorious British official named Henry Hamilton was captured and brought to town to be imprisoned. Hamilton was called "Hair-buyer" because he had alledgedly paid Indians for the scalps of Continental soldiers. All through the war, Virginia's forces

had been fighting Indian Nations that were often allies of Great Britain. The Nations were angry because Americans were taking more and more of their territory from them. It was yet more conflict for the continent.

In 1779, Thomas Jefferson became the new governor of Virginia, and soon after, Williamsburg lost its status as capital city. About 40 miles up the James River, the new capital of Richmond was closer to the growing settlements in the west and safer from British attack. Some of Williamsburg's businesses moved to Richmond, and the old colonial town lost its former bustle and energy. Would history now pass Williamsburg by?

The most powerful weapon in the Revolution was the cannon, but the Americans had far fewer than the British.

Reading History's Clues

Williamsburg's archaeologists and historians are constantly uncovering sites and making discoveries about the colonial past. In the past several years, they've been working on an important new archaeological site just outside the gates to the Capitol. Richard Charlton's Coffeehouse was a place where the town's leading gentlemen met to discuss business, news, and the political situation over coffee, hot chocolate, or wine.

When archaeologists excavated the backyard, they found a real treasure trove: a trash midden or pit dating to the time the coffeehouse was open. Careful excavation and sifting through the trash heap provided over 70,000 artifacts and animal bones. These have helped scholars understand more about how Charlton set his table and the food he served. The high style of both the food and the tableware suggest the coffeehouse attracted well-to-do gentry.

After the excavations were complete, reconstruction of the site began. Colonial Williamsburg's archaeologists, historians, and artisans have all been involved in this project, the first major reconstruction on Duke of Gloucester Street in 50 years. The new Charlton's looks and feels like the old. A central chimney, constructed of bricks made by Colonial Williamsburg artisans, rises from the basement and serves seven fireplaces. Guests to Charlton's will find the kind of fine furnishings, maps, prints, and newspapers that the colonial gentry would have expected in a coffeehouse, not to mention steaming cups of coffee and chocolate.

Costumed tradesmen work on rebuilding Charlton's Coffeehouse using tools and methods from the 1700s. Today's artisans make nails, bricks, and other materials in much the same way colonial workmen did.

A Hard-won Victory

The spring and summer of 1780 were tense times for the people of Williamsburg and for all Virginians. They were getting ready for the war to come to them at last. The Continental forces had been fighting British Commander Lord Cornwallis and his troops in the South, but the redcoats had turned north. In October a British invasion force sailed into the Chesapeake Bay. When it was called south to reinforce Cornwallis, Virginians breathed a sigh of relief. But five weeks later the British returned under the command of Benedict Arnold.

The patriots hated Arnold because he was a traitor. He had first been an outstanding American officer but later agreed to sneak valuable information to the British. Now he was commanding an army moving against Virginia. By January 5, 1781, Arnold's forces had sailed up the James River and invaded Richmond. They stayed only a day and burned two warehouses and an important foundry where military supplies were made. Governor Jefferson was relieved they didn't do any more damage, saying, "We have escaped to a miracle."

In the last year of the Revolution, the Palace Green (opposite) bustled with activity as thousands of British, French, and American troops marched in and out of town. The British general Cornwallis considered a full attack on Williamsburg to trap Continental forces there, but he decided against it. A spiked fence around the Magazine (above) helped protect the American guns and ammunition inside.

The turncoat Benedict Arnold, who had first served in the Continental Army, marched into Williamsburg as a general leading British forces in the spring of 1781, but he didn't stay long.

But Arnold didn't go away. According to documents historians have uncovered, on April 20 he "landed with part of the army at Williamsburg." They stayed for two days before moving on. The Americans sent their French ally, the Marquis de Lafayette, to Virginia to defeat Arnold, but Lord Cornwallis came up from the South to reinforce him. Clearly, a major battle was brewing. Jefferson wrote to George Washington, warning, "Arms and a naval force… are what must ultimately save us. This movement of our Enemies we consider as most perilous."

On June 25, 1781, Cornwallis's army arrived in Williamsburg and filled the town with redcoats. One townsman, St. George Tucker, wrote that "with them pestilence and famine took root, and poverty brought up the rear….The British plundered all that they could." The army also brought swarms of biting flies with them. "It is impossible to eat, drink, sleep, write, sit still or even walk about in peace," Tucker said. They stayed for ten days before marching farther down to the James. Some slaves, seeing this as a chance for freedom, marched with them.

Soon after the British left, the forces of the Marquis de Lafayette appeared. Suddenly, Williamsburg was at the heart of the Revolution again. On September 14, George Washington and two French generals arrived to plan battle tactics with Lafayette. The war was reaching an important moment.

By now, Cornwallis was in the port of Yorktown, about ten miles from Williamsburg, and at the end of September, the Continental and French forces marched toward him. Among those forces were African-American men. At first, Washington had refused to let them into the army, but as the war dragged on, he changed his mind. Now, some slaves as well as free blacks were fighting for the patriot cause. Their service did not mean they would be given freedom, so without records historians can only guess at the reasons they chose to fight.

Cornwallis's men had dug fortifications in the earth around Yorktown to protect their positions. Washington's men began digging their own in a zigzag pattern that would get them closer and closer to the British. For three weeks the Americans bombarded the British, and the redcoats fought back.

On the night of October 14, American soldiers crept up on the British for an assault and took control of two of their defensive posts. With his army in danger, Cornwallis tried to ferry his troops across the York River to safety. When a storm stopped him, he knew the end had come.

On October 19, American and British troops met on a field in Yorktown, not to do battle but to take part in an amazing moment in history—the British surrender. "The French troops, in complete uniform, displayed a martial and noble appearance," a doctor with the Continental Army wrote. "The Americans, though not all in uniform, nor their dress so neat, yet exhibited an erect, soldierly air, and every countenance beamed with satisfaction and joy." The great British Empire had been beaten, and the story passed down was that the British fife and drum corps played "The World Turned Upside Down." But historians have found no documentation for that. Instead, they know the Americans played their own popular tune, "Yankee Doodle." With the victory at Yorktown, the American colonies had won their cherished independence.

American soldiers and civilians gathered on Surrender Field to watch the British forces lay down their arms. Some fighting went on after the victory at Yorktown, but the British never recovered from their loss here.

CONCLUSION:
BIRTH OF A NATION

*I*n a lot of ways the American Revolution changed the course of world history. When the colonists declared their right to independence in 1776, they set an example for other people throughout the world to follow. Now, almost 250 years later, we sometimes take for granted the courage it took to break away from the mother country.

Williamsburg fueled much of that courage. It was here that many of the Revolution's most prominent thinkers and orators began considering the idea of freedom for America. Did the colonies have to be under British rule forever, or did human beings have the right to decide their own destinies, without interference from a king or faraway parliament? To the British, these were treasonous thoughts. The patriots who preached them could have been hanged, but they had the courage to speak out anyway.

The Revolution was long and hard, and many soldiers gave up the fight. Even those who weren't involved directly in the war—the citizens of Williamsburg and other cities, towns, and farms—had to do without things they needed. They died of disease and lived in fear of the British. But their suffering paid off. After the long years of war, America won its independence and went on to establish an entirely new nation and system of government, where "life, liberty, and the pursuit of happiness" were considered birthrights—for some. Sadly, it would take almost another hundred years and another war before African Americans would be granted those same freedoms.

Washington's Continental Army flag was the patriots' banner before the American flag was designed. Its 13 stripes stood for the 13 colonies, and the British Union Jack appeared in the field of blue.

Bringing the Past to Life

In the early 20th century Williamsburg was a quiet but dignified little town, despite what one visitor described as the "shabbiness of its houses." Local residents seemed to like the slow pace of their village. One mayor described it this way: "Williamsburg on a summer day! The straggling street, ankle deep in dust, grateful only to the chickens, ruffling their feathers in perfect safety from any traffic danger. The cows taking refuge from the heat of the sun, under the elms along the sidewalk."

After World War I, more and more people decided that old buildings should be saved, and the historic preservation movement was born. The rector of Bruton Parish Church, Dr. W. A. R. Goodwin, came to believe that the entire town should be restored.

John D. Rockefeller, Jr., saw what Goodwin saw, that if the town were restored, "unparalleled vistas" would "open into the nation's past." In 1926, Rockefeller agreed to help fund the restoration of the entire colonial town!

Now, after more than 80 years, hundreds of colonial buildings have been restored or reconstructed on their original sites. They include homes, taverns, stores, and the workshops of silversmiths, wheelwrights, and blacksmiths, as well as the grand Governor's Palace and the Capitol. Curators have collected original 18th-century objects to fill the sites. And where that hasn't been possible, talented artisans have re-created the kinds of bricks, metal objects, and furnishings these homes would have had in the colonial era. The work of Colonial Williamsburg's archaeologists, historians, and preservationists isn't just about restoring buildings, though. It also helps us understand what life was like 250 years ago.

Goodwin was right. The restoration of Colonial Williamsburg has opened unparalleled vistas into the nation's past.

At Colonial Williamsburg, the past is brought to life with incredible attention to detail. Colonial gardening methods are replicated (top left), and so are colonial modes of travel (top right). The colonial clothing worn by interpreters is made painstakingly by hand (bottom left). All this gives visitors a chance to be witnesses to history—or just to have fun (bottom right).

PORTRAYING A SLAVE

Jared Armstead, 15 (below, holding the mirror), is in his third season working as one of Colonial Williamsburg's junior interpreters. "I feel a little awkward playing the role of a slave," he says, "but it's worth it, because it really shows visitors how things were back then. Slaves worked for their owners from sunup to sundown, six days a week, then on Sundays they had to work on their own gardens." His favorite parts of the job have been learning about carpentry and about the way people lived in the colonial era.

Chronology

1607: English colonists arrive on the coast of Virginia and build a fort they call Jamestown on the James River, both named in honor of their king.

1693: King William and Queen Mary charter a new college named after them at Middle Plantation, several miles from Jamestown.

1698: The Virginia Statehouse in Jamestown burned down. Many people think the colonial capital should be moved to a healthier location away from the swamps of Jamestown, and the next year, the General Assembly directs that a new capital city named Williamsburg be built at Middle Plantation.

1754–1763: Colonial troops, including an officer named George Washington, join British forces to fight the French and their Indian allies in the French and Indian War. It is part of a larger conflict between the French and British called the Seven Years War.

1764–1765: The British Parliament passes several new laws, including the Stamp Act, which tax the colonists. The colonists protest with the cry "No taxation without representation." Patrick Henry gives his famous Caesar-Brutus speech against King George in Williamsburg.

1768: The Treaty of Fort Stanwix is signed with Iroquois Indians.

In it, the Indians give up vast amounts of territory in New York, Pennsylvania, and Virginia.

1769: Royal Governor Botetourt dissolves the Virginia General Assembly because the burgesses adopt a resolution that only they have the right to levy taxes in Virginia.

1771: Lord Dunmore becomes royal governor of Virginia.

1773: A Committee of Correspondence is established by the Virginia House of Burgesses. It encourages the legislatures of all the colonies to communicate with each other their growing concerns about the British.

1774: Williamsburg observes a day of "fasting, humilitition, and prayer" because the British have closed Boston Harbor after colonists dressed as Indians threw British tea into the harbor to protest a new law. Several months later, the First Continental Congress convenes in Philadelphia.

1775: Lord Dunmore orders the colony's gunpowder removed from the Williamsburg Magazine by British sailors. Citizens are furious. Two months later, Dunmore slips out of Williamsburg and begins living shipboard, moving along Virginia's rivers. He begins raids on patriot strongholds and issues an emancipation proclamation, promising to free "all indented Servants, Negroes, or others" belonging to patriots and willing to join the

British. In Massachusetts the first shots of the Revolution are fired.

1776: Virginia's legislature directs its delegates to the Second Continental Congress to propose that the colonies become independent. Virginia adopts its own Declaration of Rights, which influences the Declaration of Independence adopted a month later by the Continental Congress. Patrick Henry becomes the first non-royal governor of Virginia. Under the new constitution of the independent Commonwealth of Virginia, Henry serves two one-year terms.

1779: Thomas Jefferson, who wrote most of the Declaration of Independence, is elected the second governor of Virginia. The war continues in the North.

1780: Virginia's capital is moved up the James River to Richmond.

1781: The war comes to Virginia, and British and Continental troops occupy Williamsburg. In October, after weeks of heavy fighting in nearby Yorktown, the British surrender to the Americans. It marks the unofficial end of the Revolution, but the war officially ends when the Treaty of Paris is ratified in 1783; news reaches Williamsburg in early 1784.

Index

Illustrations are indicated by **boldface.**

American Revolution
    British surrender 41, **41**
    impact on slaves 30
    impact on townspeople **8,** 29–30
    northern battles 21, 29
Archaeology 36
Armstead, Jared 45, **45**
Arnold, Benedict 39–40, **40**
Artisans 30, **36–37,** 44

Bill of Rights 27
Blacksmiths 23, **23,** 29, **29,** 30
Boston Tea Party 20
Brafferton School 17
Bray School 15
British
    Army in Williamsburg **20,** 40, **40**
    northern losses 33–34
    surrender 41, **41**
    taxes on colonists 19, 20
    ties to Williamsburg 14
Bruton Parish Church 11, **13,** 44

Capitol Building **10,** 12
Chamber pots **34**
Charlton's Coffeehouse 36, **36–37**
Cherokee Indians **16–17**
Children 15, 17, **31, 32,** 33, **33**
Cobbler **15**
College of William and Mary 9, 11, 17
Colonists 19–20
Committees of Correspondence 19–20
Continental Army **8, 22,** 23–25, 29,
        33–34
    flag 25, **42,** 43
Continental Congresses 20, 23, 25
Cornwallis, Lord 39, 40–41

Declaration of Independence 25, **25**
Declaration of Rights **26,** 27
Duke of Gloucester Street **10,** 12
Dunmore, Lord 20, 21, 23, 24, 29

Flags 25, **42,** 43
France, alliance with Americans 34, 40, 41

Gentry 9, 12, 14
George III, King (Great Britain) 19, 23
Goodwin, W. A. R. 44
Great Hopes Plantation **31, 33**

Hamilton, Henry 34
Henry, Patrick 19, **19,** 20, 30
House of Burgesses 19, 20
Hurricanes 23

Indentured servants 12–13

Indians 9, **16–17,** 17, 25, 30, 34–35
Interpreters **4–5,** 9, **45**

Jamestown, Virginia 11
Jefferson, Thomas 14, 25, 35, 39, 40

Lafayette, Marquis de 40
Loyalists **20,** 20–21, **21**

Magazine **20,** 21, **39**
Maps 14
Market Square **11,** 12
Mason, George 27
Merchants 12, 29–30
Middle Plantation 11
Middling class 14–15
Milliner **28**

Palace Green **38**
Pamphlet, Gowan **30**
Patriots 21, 23, 24, 25, 43
Powhatan Indians 17

Randolph, Peyton 20
Richmond, Virginia 35, 39
Rockefeller, John D., Jr. 44

Saratoga, New York 33–34
Schools 9, 15, 17
Shoes **15, 34**
Slaves
    childhood 15, **32,** 33
    churches **13,** 30
    crossing from Africa 9, 13
    daily life **12, 18, 24,** 30, **31,** 33, 45

denial of rights 25, 27, 30
education 15
impact of Revolution on 30
as indentured servants 12–13
interpreters 45, **45**
sales sign **13**
seeking freedom 15, 24, 40
separation of families 21, **21,** 30
as soldiers 24, 40
Social classes 14–15
Stamp Act 19
Surrender Field **41**

Tar and feathers **20**
Taxes 19, 20
Tucker, St. George 40

Virginia Convention 20, 27
Virginia Declaration of Rights **26,** 27
Virginia General Assembly 30
Voting rights 30

Washington, George 23, 25, 40–41, 43
Weapons 23, **25, 34–35, 39**
Williamsburg, Virginia
    as colonial capital 11
    early growth 12
    restoration 44
    revolutionary ideas 43
    ties to Britain 14
Women **12,** 25, 30, 36

Yorktown, Virginia 40–41

SELECTED BIBLIOGRAPHY

Albion's Seed: Four British Folkways in America, by David Hackett Fischer, Oxford University Press, 1989.
Becoming Americans: Our Struggle to Be Both Free and Equal, edited by Cary Carson, The Colonial
    Williamsburg Foundation, 2002.
A Chronology of Virginia and the War of Independence 1763-1783, by John E. Selby, Virginia
    Independence Bicentennial Commission, University Press of Virginia, 1976.
The Revolution in Virginia: 1775-1783, by John E. Selby, The Colonial Williamsburg Foundation, 1988.
Slavery and Freedom in the Age of the American Revolution, edited by Ira Berlin and Ronald
    Hoffman, University of Virginia Press, 1983.
Williamsburg Before and After: The Rebirth of Virginia's Colonial Capital, by George Humphrey
    Yetter, The Colonial Williamsburg Foundation, 1988.
Primary Sources: *The Papers of Thomas Jefferson, Vol. 1-6,* edited by Julian Boyd et al, Princeton
    University Press, 1950-52.
Revolutionary Virginia: The Road to Independence, Compiled and edited by Robert L. Scribner and
    Brent Tarter, Virginia Independence Bicentennial Commission, University Press of Virginia, 1976.
"'Releese us out of this Cruell Bondegg': An Appeal from Virginia in 1723." Ingersoll, Thomas
    N. *William & Mary Quarterly,* Third Series, Vol. 51, No. 4.
The Avalon Project: Documents in Law, History and Diplomacy. http://avalon.law.yale.edu/
The online database www.slavevoyages.org provides information on the slave trade in the Americas.
Colonial Williamsburg's website offers a variety of research materials.
    Go to http://research.history.org/ and choose Research.

To my mother, Helen, who taught me to love history and so much more ❧ *KMK*

For my dad, William, who taught me to use his camera. For my mom, Barbara, who taught me to be independent. And for my husband, Scott, who teaches me about love every day ❧ *LER*

Acknowledgments: My deepest thanks to Paul Aron, Managing Editor of Publications for Colonial Williamsburg. He gave me my own new look at Williamsburg and guided me to the stellar staff of historians, artisans, and interpreters who have spent their lives preserving the history and essence of Colonial Williamsburg. Among the many who helped me, a special thanks to historians Linda Rowe, for her knowledge and patience, and Kevin Kelly and Cathleene Hellier for their expertise. Thanks also to Joseph Rountree, Amy Watson, Jae White, and Julie Watson. To my National Geographic colleagues on this book, my heartfelt appreciation goes to Jennifer Emmett for her keen vision and guidance and to Lori Renda and Jim Hiscott, whose talents have made this book what it is.—KMK

All photos by Lori Epstein Renda unless otherwise noted below:
Colonial Williamsburg: 13 bottom, 26-27, 42, 45 bottom left; David M. Doody: 2-3, 6-7, 11, 16-17, 19, 20 top, 22, 25 top, 30, 34-35, 39; Barbara Temple Lombardi: 38, 40, 41 bottom.

PUBLISHED BY THE NATIONAL GEOGRAPHIC SOCIETY
John M. Fahey, Jr., *President and Chief Executive Officer*
Gilbert M. Grosvenor, *Chairman of the Board*
Tim T. Kelly, President, *Global Media Group*
John Q. Griffin, *Executive Vice President; President, Publishing*
Nina D. Hoffman, *Executive Vice President; President, Book Publishing Group*
Melina Gerosa Bellows, *Executive Vice President, Children's Publishing*

PREPARED BY THE BOOK DIVISION
Nancy Laties Feresten, *Vice President, Editor in Chief, Children's Books*
Bea Jackson, *Director of Design and Illustrations, Children's Books*
Amy Shields, *Executive Editor, Series, Children's Books*
Jennifer Emmett, *Executive Editor, Reference and Solo, Children's Books*
Carl Mehler, *Director of Maps;* R. Gary Colbert, *Production Director*
Jennifer A. Thornton, *Managing Editor*

STAFF FOR THIS BOOK
Jennifer Emmett, *Editor;* James Hiscott, Jr., *Art Director/Designer*
Lori Renda, *Illustrations Editor;* Matt Chwastyk, *Map Production*
Grace Hill, *Associate Managing Editor;* Lewis R. Bassford, *Production Manager;* Susan Borke, *Legal and Business Affairs*

MANUFACTURING AND QUALITY MANAGEMENT
Christopher A. Liedel, *Chief Financial Officer;* Phillip L. Schlosser, *Vice President;* Chris Brown, *Technical Director;* Nicole Elliott, *Manager;* Rachel Faulise, *Manager*

For more information, please call 1-800-NGS LINE (647-5463) or write to the following address:
National Geographic Society
1145 17th Street N.W.
Washington, D.C. 20036-4688 U.S.A.

Visit us online at www.nationalgeographic.com/books
For librarians and teachers: www.ngchildrensbooks.org
More for kids from National Geographic:
kids.nationalgeographic.com
For information about special discounts for bulk purchases, please contact National Geographic Books Special Sales:
ngspecsales@ngs.org
For rights or permissions inquiries, please contact National Geographic Books Subsidiary Rights: ngbookrights@ngs.org

Front Cover: Though George Washington was at first reluctant to allow it, eventually both free blacks and slaves fought for the Continental Army during the Revolutionary War. ***Back cover (top to bottom):*** Scenes from a city at war—Kids played while soldiers patrolled; wealthy families entertained even as times grew tough; slaves were wrenched from family and friends when their masters left town. ***p. 1*** A fife and drum corps march through the streets of Colonial Williamsburg. ***p. 4-5*** Aim, steady, fire! Smoke plumes from a flintlock musket.

Library of Congress Cataloging-in-Publication Data
Kostyal, K. M., 1951-
  1776 : a new look at revolutionary Williamsburg / by K.M. Kostyal with the Colonial Williamsburg Foundation; photographs by Lori Epstein Renda.
    p. cm.
  Includes bibliographical references and index.
   ISBN 978-1-4263-0517-7 (hardcover : alk. paper) -- ISBN 978-1-4263-0518-4 (library binding : alk. paper)
   1. Williamsburg (Va.)--History--Revolution, 1775-1783--Juvenile literature. I. Epstein Renda, Lori, ill. II. Colonial Williamsburg Foundation. III. Title. IV. Title: Seventeen seventy-six.
   F234.W7K677 2009
   973.3'1097554252--dc22
                                      2009018002

Printed in the United States of America

09/WOR/1